TONY HADLEY

my life in pictures

For Tom, Toni, Mack,
Zara and Genevieve
– with love xxxxx

TONY HADLEY

my life in pictures

OMNIBUS PRESS

London / New York / Paris / Sydney / Copenhagen / Berlin / Madrid / Tokyo

Hi everyone!

I'M SO EXCITED to share this photographic trip down memory lane: an exclusive 'access all areas' look at my life through the lens.

Celebrating forty years in the music business got me thinking about all the fantastic experiences I've had in my career. As the memories came flooding back, I reached for my photo albums and have had such a good time looking through hundreds of images that capture some really great events – and also just me and my friends having fun! I've gone down a nostalgic and emotional path reminiscing on the wonderful adventures that have a special place in my heart, from fronting one of the biggest pop groups of the 80s, to an incredible solo career that's taken me around the world.

As you know, music is my passion and I am so fortunate to have a successful career doing something I love. Growing up in Islington in London, I always loved music and was weaned on it by my mum, Jo, and my dad, Pat. Although I was into pop, reggae and punk, my parents' love of swing – Frank Sinatra, Tony Bennett, Jack Jones and many others – had a profound influence on me and my style of singing. Every Sunday morning, whilst Mum prepared lunch, my siblings and I would hear this wonderful music blasting out from our parents' record player!

I sang in the school church choir and at the Guildhall in London, but despite my early love of singing I never envisaged that performing in front of thousands of people would become my vocation. In fact, my first passion was medicine; I dearly wanted to be an orthopaedic surgeon. At one stage I even flirted with the idea of joining the military, but I found music instead. Winning a singing competition at a Pontins holiday camp aged 14 was the turning point and the rest, as they say, is history…

I have gathered many photos of stage performances and backstage antics but there's so much more to this book than the gigs. What I do for a living has afforded me so many other opportunities, which I am incredibly grateful for. It's an honour to have entertained our British, NATO and UN troops on active service around the world in places most people never get to visit, such as the Falkland Islands, Ascension Island and Kuwait.

Over the years I've been privileged to be able to support many charities and I'm especially proud to work closely with Shooting Star Children's Hospices, Action Medical Research, Huntington's Disease Association and others.

I've also stepped out of my comfort zone to star on the West End stage playing Billy Flynn in *Chicago* and appeared on *I'm a Celebrity… Get Me Out of Here*.

Unearthing picture after picture has been a real joy and I wanted to share the snaps and the stories behind them with you all, and the many of you who have followed me over the years. Hopefully these photographs will not only give you an insight into my life but will also trigger some amazing and happy memories of your own. I hope you enjoy seeing them as much as I have enjoyed revisiting them. Of course, the journey doesn't stop here and I'm looking forward to many more years of working and touring with my band, known as The Fabulous TH Band.

I've been so fortunate in life. It can sometimes be very lonely in this business and I'm thankful for the support of my family and friends through the good times and the bad. I'm blessed with five beautiful children, Tom, Toni, Mackenzie, Zara and Genevieve, who mean the world to me. Finally, thank you to my darling wife, Ali, for her love and support. I love you all very much.

Tony Hadley, 2022

THE IMAGES

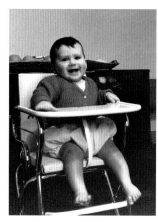

EARLY YEARS

Going through the boxes of precious photographs from my childhood has been bittersweet. The pictures brought back lots of wonderful and funny memories, but it also made me sad remembering loved ones I've lost.

[Left] Here's my dad, Pat, when he was in his 20s, looking rather handsome, don't you think? My lovely mum, Jo, took the photo whilst they were on holiday. It was the mid-1950s and my parents loved travelling, which in those days was quite adventurous; they were a very modern couple. My dad was an amazing man and a fabulous friend to many; he left a huge hole in all our lives when he sadly died aged just 63 following a heart attack. This picture is very special to me. Dad was an electrical engineer for the *Daily Mail* and I used to go down to Fleet Street in London to see him in the machine rooms, which I loved. He was taken from us far too soon. I'm so sad that he wasn't able be part of so many special moments in my life.

Here's my mum and dad with my maternal grandmother, Nan Rose, at the seaside. My nan died of cancer when she was 67 and I was just 17. She was the first person in the family that I had lost, and it knocked me for six. I was extremely close to her; I could talk to her about anything. When I told her I wanted to go into the music business she was so supportive but made me promise to never take drugs and I never have.

[Right, from top] I love this picture with Nan Rose. I was born in 1960 and I'm just a couple of months old here. We were a close-knit north London family; we lived at Percy Circus, Islington, Nan and Grandad Bill lived around the corner, and I had aunts and uncles living close by too. It was like that back in those days, extended families living very near each other. Growing up, there was always someone to turn to if you needed anything, but there was also always someone spying on you if you got up to no good!

These baby and toddler photos are sweet. I look very happy. It was probably because I was spoilt rotten. I was the first baby in the immediate family and I must have had a lot of attention.

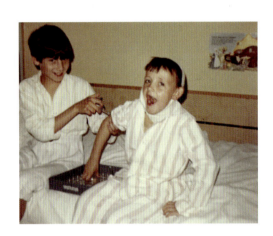

EARLY YEARS

These school year pictures have bought back a real mixed bag of memories. [Left, clockwise] I was 10 years old in the picture of me in hospital, playing the clown with a boy I'd just met. I had been on a school trip to Norfolk when I banged my leg mucking about on the bunk beds. The next morning, when we were leaving, I could hardly get out of bed. My leg was killing me; I was in agony. When I got home I couldn't walk, so my parents took me to A&E at the Royal Free Hospital. The doctors said it was bruising and a bit of swelling, and we were sent home. At three o'clock in the morning I woke screaming in excruciating pain and was rushed back to hospital. Luckily I was seen by a consultant very quickly. It turned out I had osteomyelitis, which is a swelling that occurs as a result of infection. Basically I had sepsis. I was pumped full of antibiotics, had emergency surgery the next day and was in hospital for two months, followed by crutches for three months, a walking stick for two months and no sport for two years. I didn't know it at the time but I was only an hour away from dying. I was in recovery in this picture and didn't realise the seriousness of my condition. I'm lucky to be here today.

I'm dressed up for Christmas day with my brother, Steve, who is five years younger than me, and my sister, Lee, who is two years younger. I love my matching shirt and tie! That was a definite look back then. My mum probably bought the outfits at Chapel Market in Islington.

The pool photo is at a Pontins holiday camp. There are Lee and Steve and childhood friends Kerry and Jill Henry. They lived around the corner, on Great Percy Street. Kerry and I were in the same class and their mum Maureen became great friends with my mum, and they still are to this day.

[Right] This picture is probably the only one that exists of me performing at Pontins with the house band. I probably sang 'Young Girl' or 'You Are the Sunshine of My Life'. I was 15 or 16, and it was around the time I was involved in forming a band at school. Cutting my teeth on stage at Pontins paved the way for the start of my music career.

The school photo on page 7 is a classic headshot taken when I was around 9 or 10 years old. Clerkenwell Parochial School was fantastic, though it was pretty primitive with outside toilets and coke boilers in all the classrooms which the caretaker filled every morning. I liked my teachers and enjoyed my school days; it was a very happy time for me. The haircut is a bit severe, though. Dad used to take us to the local Greek or Italian barbers and the result was pretty dodgy. He also once purchased something he saw in an advert that was essentially a razor blade within a comb. It promised to save you money on haircuts, but it was brutally painful, so he soon got rid of that.

GENTRY, 1979

Spandau Ballet was born out of our school band, Gentry. This line-up went on to become one of the biggest bands of the 80s with me, Gary Kemp, Martin Kemp and Steve Norman. We all went to Dame Alice Owen's School in Potters Bar.

I had always been into music and singing so getting into a band at school was the next step. I was a frustrated drummer (and still am) and was drumming away in the music room one day when in walked Gary, John and Steve, and a few others, who had formed a band. John immediately kicked me off the drums and started playing, and of course he was amazing. A couple of girls were singing with the band, but it didn't really work. Steve told me they were looking for a lead singer. I sang something a cappella – and the rest is history. We had a number of different names and personnel at first. We had Michael Ellison on bass in our first band, Roots, and Richie Miller when we were The Cut and The Makers, before Martin finally joined us as the bass guitarist in Spandau Ballet.

Even as a fledgling band we were quite savvy and publicity aware. We asked mates to take our picture and got posters made. We started off playing gigs in well-known venues such as The Golden Lion in Fulham and The Greyhound in Hammersmith. We even played upstairs at Ronnie Scott's in Soho and supported the Tom Robinson Band at The Sir George Robey in Finsbury. We were determined to get our faces seen by as many people as possible.

These were the first pictures taken of Gentry. We're at Lincoln's Inn Fields, a public square in London. We were getting recognised and were beginning to grow in confidence and direction. I was about 17 years old. When you're in a band you need to be very determined. You've got to live and breathe it and have faith in yourselves. Throw in talent and you've got a good chance of success. I knew we would get some knockbacks along the way, but we honestly felt that we were going to be something big.

LONDON, 1979

Our first appearance as Spandau Ballet, this performance was the start of our meteoric rise to stardom. As a school band we had changed names five times – we were Roots, The Cut, The Makers then Gentry – before we became Spandau Ballet.

We were already known on the club scene, but an invitation-only event held at Halligan's Studio on London's Holloway Road in November was our springboard to fame.

We played in front of the major influencers of the day, the shapers of the New Romantic scene, young artists, fashionistas, designers, entrepreneurs. We passed their test and the following month had our first gig at the Blitz club, the uber cool hangout for London's glitterati. From that moment Spandau Ballet were on their way.

LONDON, 1979
This was taken in a really horrible squat in London's Warren Street. There were a bunch of 'Blitz kids' hanging out there, such as Steve Strange and fashion designers Melissa Caplan and Stephen Linard – real shapers of the 80s youth movement. I love this image.

LONDON, 1980

I think these pictures are hilarious. I look like a member of the clergy in the headshot! Looking back, the outfits were bizarre, but that was the point! The more outrageous the better. Believe it or not, I used to walk around London looking like this; we didn't just dress up for photoshoots. I would go to Chapel Market dressed up to the nines.

My grandad, Bill, had a name for those baggy trousers and it wasn't very flattering! My grandad was a class act; he always wore a three-piece suit and perfectly shined shoes, knew all the faces in London and was well respected. One day I met him at Waterloo station as we were going to meet my mum, dad, Lee and Steve, who were on holiday on the south coast. I had on baggy trousers, a frilly shirt and ballet slippers! He said, 'If you think I'm getting on a train with you dressed like that, you can think again.' He refused to sit in the same carriage as me!

UE GAMBETTA · S! TROPEZ ☎ 97·01·78

SAINT-TROPEZ, 1980
(THIS PAGE AND PREVIOUS SPREAD)

The band was very much in demand and being courted
by all the major record companies. We were invited
to play a two-week residency at Le Papagayo, a very
exclusive, upmarket nightclub in Saint-Tropez. Playing
live nightly was a great way to cut our teeth in the
music business.

We met up outside my mum and dad's house,
crammed everything we needed into a hire car and
set off. We were squashed, packed to the rafters with
suitcases on the roof, but we didn't care – we were off
to Saint-Tropez.

I shared the driving with John and on my shift a tyre
blew. We careered wildly across the busy road towards
the oncoming traffic. Fortunately I just managed to
swerve back in time, but it was pretty scary. That was
the second time in my life that I nearly didn't make it!

After flagging down a truck to help us get back on
the road, we were soon soaking up the glitz of Saint-
Tropez. We drank ourselves silly on the first night
and ran up a £3,000 bar bill. We thought we'd hit the
jackpot! We hoped to be staying in a swanky villa, but
it was a grotty apartment block with mattresses on the
floor. Not quite as glamorous as we had imagined!

TARIF CONSOMMATIONS
ANS
APÉRITIFS
AMERS - AMERCANO
PORTO
MARTINI-GIN
GIN FIZZ
COCA RHUM
   GIN
   COGNAC
DEMI
BIÈRE
BIÈRES ÉTRANGÈRES
PERRIER - EAUX MINÉRALES
SODAS
TONIC - BITTER - GINI
CITRON-ORANGE PRESSÉS
JUS DE FRUIT
SIROPS PUR SUCRE
LIQUEURS DE MARQUE
COGNAC RHUM
ALCOOLS BLANC
VODKA
   - ORANGE
WHISKY
CAFÉ
CAFÉ CRÈME - CHOCOLAT
ORANGE
THÉ - INFUSIONS
LAIT NATURE
LAIT SIROP

SAINT-TROPEZ, 1980

We performed short sets, mostly original stuff from *Journeys to Glory*. We went down a storm. It was an exciting time, having photographers and an entourage following us every night. We played late, stayed up even later having drinks and then at 4 am we'd buy freshly baked chocolate croissants from the baker around the corner from the bar. The smell was divine.

LONDON, 1980

I really like the composition of this shot, taken during a photoshoot at The Waldorf Hotel, London. On the fashion front, we were always looking for a new image, staying one step ahead of the trends. This outfit was designed for me by Melissa Caplan, who was very cutting edge with her work.

LONDON, 1980

What a momentous occasion! I was 20 years old and signing my first recording contract, with Chrysalis, at their office in London.

From forming the school band in 1976 to this moment, there had been four years of hard work, playing every pub and club gig possible.

When you love music all you want to do is play and the ambition is to be signed by a record label. We'd made it; I felt euphoric. We went out after and drank bottles and bottles of champagne. I had never drunk champagne before – it was quite a step up from lager! That afternoon I laid down the vocal for what was to be our first top five single in the UK, 'To Cut a Long Story Short'.

LONDON, 1980

We had entered the whirlwind world of photoshoots, press interviews, video recordings and TV appearances. The publicity wheel was spinning like mad. This significant session, shot in the London Dungeon, was to promote our first single, 'To Cut a Long Story Short'. The venue was chosen because it was dark, gritty and atmospheric, like the London club scene at the time.

Photographers Neil Mackenzie Matthews, an old schoolmate, and Graham Smith were an integral part of that scene and spent a lot of time with us. They took some of the earliest behind-the-scenes pictures of Spandau, many of which are featured in this book. They are both great guys and fantastic photographers.

These images are by Graham. When being photographed, I felt a lot more comfortable with the band beside me than on my own, but Graham handled the shoots brilliantly and always managed to get exceptional images.

We always appeared so moody and brooding in posed photos, but once the shoot was over we all started mucking about again. We were five young lads having the time of our lives. We were at the start of something very special and we were loving it.

LONDON, 1980

Graham was very experimental. I love this light-and-shade solo head shot.

LONDON, 1980

The advent of Billy's and the Blitz brought an exciting music and fashion movement to London, which was building momentum. For the 'To Cut A Long Story Short' video, we wanted to recreate that feeling of performing in a club. Clothes designer and club entrepreneur Chris Sullivan was in the video ['To Cut A Long Story Short'], along with two female regulars who danced in the background. The image was as much a part of the performance as the music. We went for quite a theatrical, military vibe, with the tartan as a nod to Soho's Le Kilt club.

Our first single reached number five in the charts, which was phenomenal.

CARDIFF, 1980

I love these backstage shots taken after a gig in Cardiff. They feel so gritty and real. The late singer Steve Strange used to get chased around the Tiger Bay area because of the way he looked. Anyone a little out of the ordinary was fair game to be mocked by the locals. That night, we got a taste of it ourselves when a load of local lads invaded the stage. We were working with the road crew to put all the gear away when we were set upon. Everything kicked off and people were getting whacked with drumsticks and anything else the crew could get hold of. It was manic. It was quite a hairy night, but we all survived.

LONDON, 1980

One of our first TV performances was playing 'To Cut a
Long Story Short' on the short-lived show *White Light*.
Every TV show is exciting… but there's an awful lot of
hanging around in dressing rooms. Nothing compares
to performing live, but we all knew the value of TV.

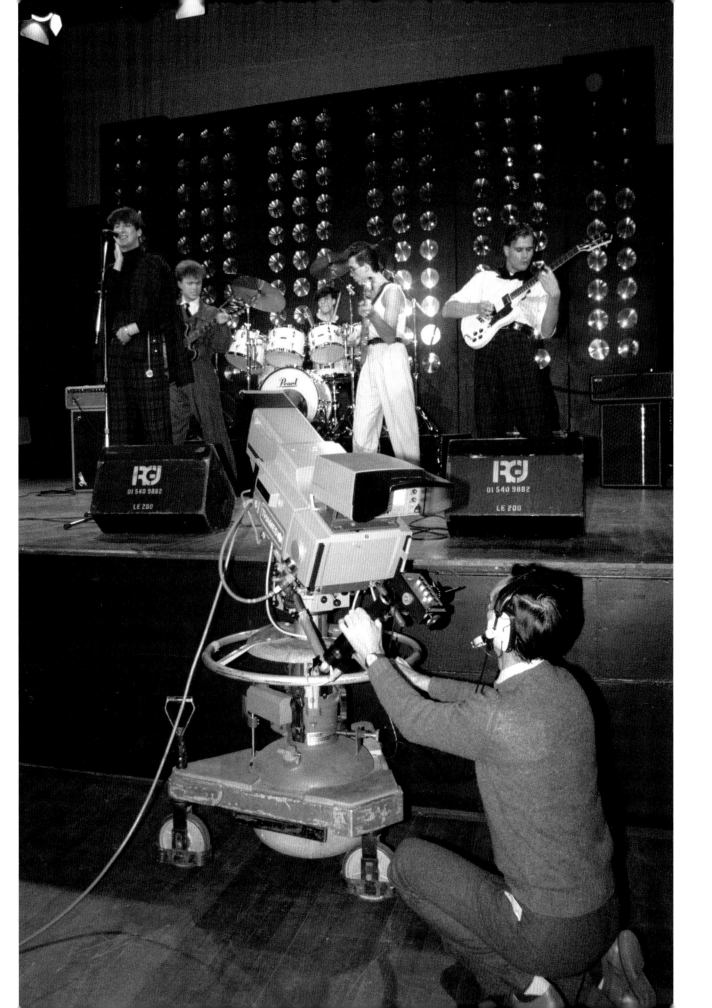

BATH, 1982 (OVERLEAF)

We were in Bath shooting the video for the single 'She Loved Like Diamond' from the second Spandau Ballet album, *Diamond*. It was a very atmospheric, misty day and I needed that big coat.

PARIS, 1982

Well, I certainly didn't need the big coat for this gig! I must have been boiling!

We didn't have a massive fanbase in France, it was more of a cult following, so we thought we would go over and try to make more of an impression. We went with a group of friends and I was there with my wife, Leonie. We met in the Blitz club when I was 19 and got married when I was 22. Despite me getting married when I was relatively young, the fans remained loyal and very supportive. Leonie and I are divorced but remain on good terms and have three wonderful children: Tom, Toni and Mackenzie.

NEW YORK, 1981 (THIS PAGE AND OVERLEAF)

I would love to know exactly what I was thinking in this shot. Maybe I couldn't believe that a 21-year-old lad from Islington was off on an all-expenses-paid trip to New York!

Chrysalis organised a packed trip to help get our name known in America. It was quite an experience, especially as I didn't know anyone who had gone to the States. As a boy I had soaked up Hollywood films and now I felt like I was on a film set – the big yellow taxis, the cops on the streets, the fire hydrants. It was loud, brash and exciting.

It was a manic week with endless rounds of photoshoots, press conferences in diners and interviews in hotel rooms. The highlight was a gig in the famous Underground club plus a fashion show. We had an entourage with us – designers, photographers, stylists – which felt very glamorous, but we still had to muck in and shift our own gear.

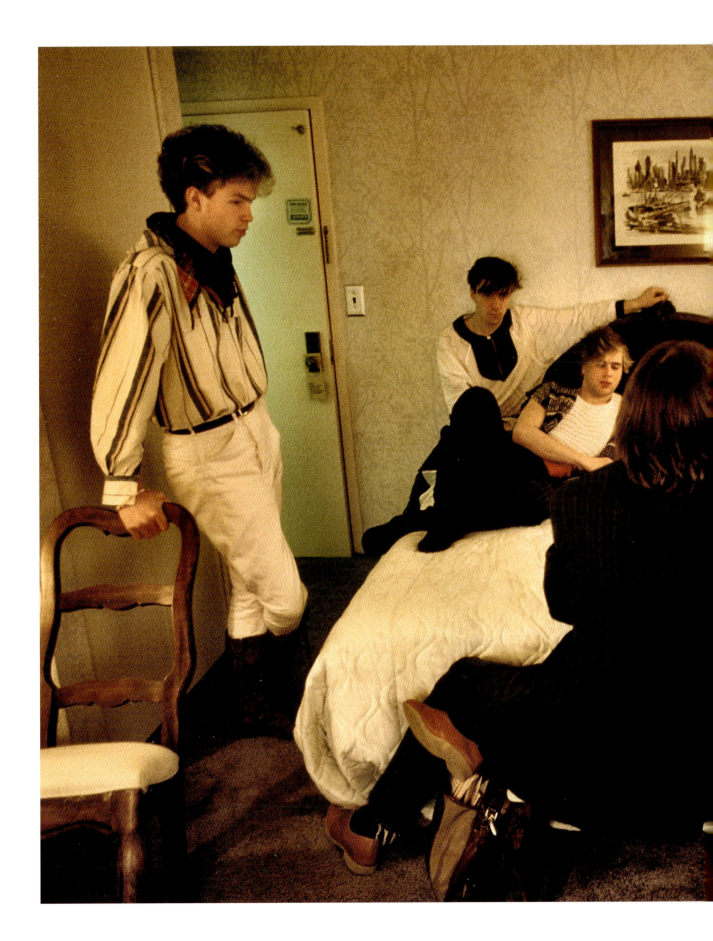

NEW YORK, 1981 (THIS PAGE AND OVERLEAF)

As well as Neil Mackenzie Matthews and Graham Smith, we had another photographer with us, Martyn Goddard. He would drive us around in a big hire car looking for locations. We'd get out and strike a pose while people stopped and stared as if we were from another planet. Even though New York seemed cutting edge, it wasn't ready for the London look!

NEW YORK, 1981
(THIS PAGE AND PREVIOUS SPREAD)

I love the shot of us eating out of paper bags. We stayed up late every night, probably missed breakfast and had to get Martyn to stop so we could grab a bite from a street stall. Everything about New York felt big and over the top. When I ordered a beef sandwich at a deli it came with eighteen slices of beef in it! I went back the next day and told the guy I only needed two slices – he thought I was mad!

The fashion show was crazy. The focus was on the designers showcasing their work, so we were more of a sideshow, but we threw ourselves into it. Ollie O'Donnell, a young hairdresser who went on to run the Le Beat Route and Wag clubs, crimped my hair before the make-up artist went to work.

It was an amazing trip but we had to wait a couple of years before we broke America, and that was down to 'True'.

IBIZA, 1981 (THIS PAGE AND OVERLEAF)

Ibiza and music have always had a close association, and we thought it would be good publicity to do a gig at the Ku Club, which was a really happening place. Lots of photographers and press came with us and loads of people flew in from London to watch the show. We were there for about a week. The record company stayed at Pikes, which is a great hotel, and we got to stay at a not-so-brilliant villa down the road.

This was a happy time for the band, and we were getting on well. We'd had some success with our first album, *Journeys to Glory*, and were happily posing around the streets of the Old Town soaking up all the attention. I think the locals thought we were a bit quirky; we thought we looked super cool. We were around 21 years old, and we couldn't believe our luck. Five young lads from Islington racing round the island in a speedboat. Although we look quite serious in the pictures, we were having a great time and a real laugh. Life was good.

BAHAMAS, 1982 (THIS PAGE AND OVERLEAF)

These photos were taken in the beautiful Bahamas, where we recorded most of the *True* album in 1982. Back then, if you recorded music abroad you got a tax break on the profits so consequently it was a very popular thing to do. We were working at Compass Point Studios in Nassau. What a great place to make an album – and with the added benefit of the beach and a pool! As well as sunbathing, I got to ride a horse along the beach, which was just amazing as a keen rider.

This was a good period for the band. We were really getting on and we felt that we had a much better album in the making of *True* compared to the previous one. We were adapting as a band and working in the Bahamas had a real influence on how we played. We didn't realise it at the time but this album was about to change our lives completely.

ROYAL ALBERT HALL, 1983

This was a fantastic time for us. We were riding high, everything was going well and the album *True* was rocketing up the charts. Our lives were changing dramatically.

The Royal Albert Hall has a special place in my heart as I met one of my musical heroes, Frank Sinatra, there in 1977. I saw him three times and on the last night I managed to wangle an introduction. He shook my hand, and I told him I was in a band and that I wanted to be a professional singer. He wished me luck; six years later I was playing on that very stage.

In 2018 I played there again and I decided to change the last song of the set to 'My Way', in homage to Sinatra. It also summed up the personal journey I have been on. It was a very emotional moment for me.

BRIGHTON, 1983

'True' went to number one in 1983. It felt like our year.

Before 'True', we weren't a 'scream teen' band; we had a more eclectic following. But suddenly the venues we were playing got bigger and we started making a bit of money. We were launched into the musical stratosphere with a massive, screaming fan base – as you can tell from this gig at Brighton's Conference Centre!

Chris Sullivan, a club entrepreneur and fashionista, was a big name on the 80s scene and he designed a lot of our outfits. He created quite a gentrified look for the 'True' period. Across the road from Chris in Kentish Town was a great tailor, Chris Ruocco, who made all our suits at the time.

LONDON, 1983

For the single 'Communication', we shot a video with the actress Leslie Ash and boxer John Conteh at the King George V Dock and Kings Cross, London – quite gritty areas back then, which suited the video perfectly. The rest of the guys weren't in it, so I was the leading role. As well as singing, there was action and dialogue; I had never acted before so was scared stiff at the prospect. Luckily Leslie and John were great, and we had a real laugh together.

   I got to drive a 3-litre Capri, get in car chases and do my own stunts so I was in my element. That was a fun day at work.

   I'm in my favourite coat from Camden Market – a German leather riding coat, which cost about £30, a lot of money back then. I still have it – it weighs a ton! I'm going to auction it for charity one day.

LONDON, 1983

Top of the Pops was celebrating its 1,000th episode at Kensington Roof Gardens and 'True' was number one in the charts. I don't know why Martin isn't in this picture as he was there!

Back then *Top of the Pops* was huge – a Thursday night must-see. Everybody in the business knew the value of the show. If you didn't go on it because you thought you were too cool, you were mad. It meant the difference between a hit and a miss. When we released 'To Cut a Long Story Short' it hovered around the high fifties, then as soon as we appeared on *TOTP* it rocketed to number five. Our record company was over the moon, along with our friends and families.

Then three years later we got our one and only number one hit. It's every band's dream to get a number one single, so it was an amazing moment. We stayed there for four weeks.

LONDON, 1984

I'm a big football fan, even if I'm not the best player
in the world. I really enjoyed being part of a team that
played for fun. We called ourselves FC El Classico
after designer Willie Brown's collection. The line-
up was (back row) Nick Egan, me, Steve Norman,
Martin Kemp, Simon Withers; (front row) Paolo
Hewitt, Christos Tolera, John Keeble, Neil Mackenzie
Matthews. Gary Kemp wasn't playing so he took the
photo, which only featured nine of us as a couple of
players were late.

For our first game we didn't have any kit, but a friend
of Neil's had merchandise for Motörhead, so we all
wore black band T-shirts! The venue was a remote
pitch just north of Crouch End, with metal goal posts,
no nets and a bumpy pitch. Not very luxurious.

I'm a north London lad and Arsenal is my
team. My nan lived in the flats overlooking the old
Highbury stadium – you could see the corner flag
from her balcony.

These were fun days, but football was never
destined to be my chosen career!

EDINBURGH, 1984

[Left] It's amazing how music can open so many doors. Here I am presenting Prince Charles with a gold disc for our hit single 'True' at a charity event for the Prince's Trust. It was a really big deal; all the band members took their parents to Edinburgh to be part of it.

My outfit was typical of the look back then: high-neck shirt, ornate brooch and silky jacket. It was a special era for fashion and music, which went hand in hand. Spending money on clothes and records was a passion of mine.

I've been involved with the Prince's Trust ever since this event. I think it's an amazing organisation and the work they do is incredible.

EDINBURGH, 1984

[Right] A bit of backstage relaxation before the gig. I'm quite a good table tennis player and also quite competitive. Not sure about playing in those leather trousers though!

LONDON, 1984

What a classic! This photo, taken at a photoshoot
to promote the Band Aid single, is very special and
perfectly captures the era.

It was the mid-80s and this was the look: big hair,
frilly shirts and ornate accessories. My white shirt was
by the Japanese designer Yohji Yamamoto. My leather
trousers were made by a dear friend of mine, Jane
Cronin, who sadly passed away. Jane made all my
leather gear, including the long coat I wore for the Live
Aid concert in 1985.

Simon Le Bon is a great guy and we go back a long
way. I think the Duran Duran boys are so very talented
and adventurous with their music. I've always been a
big fan of theirs. Paula Yates, who was Bob Geldof's
wife at the time, was so bubbly and so much fun; it was
tragic when we lost her.

LONDON, 1984

'Do They Know It's Christmas' is such an iconic record. I don't think any of us realised then just how massive Band Aid would be or how it would morph into Live Aid. Bob Geldof told us about the crisis in Africa and we all wanted to help out.

We'd been out drinking in Germany the night before with the Duran Duran boys. When we arrived at the airport on the morning of the recording we couldn't believe how many fans and paparazzi were waiting. We were all looking and feeling a bit rough but once we realised what a huge event this had become, we all rushed to make ourselves presentable.

All the big artists were there: Phil Collins, George Michael, Paul Weller, Bananarama, Boy George, Sting, Paul Young, Bono and so many more. It was an amazing day. There was no grandeur about the event. It was very much a 'biscuit and cup of tea' affair but so important; we were honoured to be involved.

LONDON, 1984

We're recording the chorus as an ensemble, and what a great line-up it was. There were around forty artists, with lots of distinct styles. I liked the fact that there were no egos on display, and we all had fun. You can't see them in this image but the wonderful Status Quo boys, Francis Rossi and the late Rick Parfitt, kept us in hysterics the whole time. They cracked us up with their antics.

LIVE AID, WEMBLEY STADIUM, 1985

Bob Geldof is showing us the Live Aid book; I'm with Midge Ure, Gary Kemp, Adam Ant and Elton John. Singing at the Live Aid concert was such a huge deal. It was so important. Wembley Stadium was heaving with more than 70,000 people and it was extremely hot. Wearing a long, double-thick leather jacket was probably not the best idea!

WEMBLEY, 1984

We played Wembley Arena and broke the house
record for the number of nights played in a row.
We played Christmas Eve, had Christmas Day off
and then were back on stage again on Boxing Day.

NEW ZEALAND, 1985

Spandau had been touring Europe for about two months during the winter and we were absolutely exhausted. We headed off down under and had ten days off in Sydney before starting our Australia/New Zealand tour. Whilst there, my one year old son Tom took his first steps at the Sebel Townhouse Hotel – what an amazing moment.

After a brilliant Australian tour, we had some time off before going to America, so my tour manager Mark and I decided to head to Auckland to see one of my favourite bands, Queen. I went to the soundcheck to say hello to the boys. Afterwards, we all went back to the hotel and Freddie Mercury said, 'Darling, would you like a drink? Let's have a vodka.' That drink led to a bottle of vodka followed by a bottle of port. This was mid-afternoon and the band was due on stage that night. Unfortunately, we were slightly blotto.

Freddie asked me if I'd like to join him on stage that evening and of course I jumped at the chance. They announced me in front of 40,000 people. During an instrumental break, Freddie threw himself on the piano and said, 'Hadley, you bastard. I'm so pissed.' I was having the time of my life, playing air guitar and trying to 'out-Fred Fred' – no one could ever do that, but I was loving it!

Freddie was a flamboyant performer but off stage he was a quiet man. He was so lovely, kind and helpful. As such an awesome frontman he gave me lots of advice. He told me, 'Remember, you're the singer, the front man, and it's your responsibility to always keep contact with the audience. Regardless of how you feel, you might be under the weather, feel sick or have a cold, you go out there and lead it.' I have always held those words close.

I was so pleased that I got to see him before he died and give him a big hug. He was such a generous man, and I was so sad when he passed away.

ITALY, 1986

This is such a moving, powerful image; the hand
reaching out is captivating.

I love this picture more for what it represents rather
than a specific moment in time. It's almost spiritual.
It's the connection between an artist and the fans. As
a singer you are touching many people's hearts when
you perform. You have to connect with your audience
and give everything you can when you're on stage. The
fans deserve it. I have been lucky enough to have such
a loyal, supportive following so I always want them to
feel that they have had a special evening when I sing.

Back in these Spandau days we hit the 'teen
scream' status. Fans would charge down the street to
try to grab us, touch our hair or take our jackets off.
It was crazy! It's so funny that some of them are still
coming to see me in concert and are now bringing
their children. I always love to meet fans and chat to
them, and I dedicate this picture to them all.

ROYAL DOCKS, 1988

(THIS PAGE AND PREVIOUS SPREAD)

We were down at the docks doing a photoshoot for the single 'Raw', which today isn't one of my favourite Spandau tracks. The day started off OK but soon went downhill, ending really badly. I had a massive row with Martin and Gary. It wasn't the best period for the band as things between us were getting very tense. It was around the recording of the album *Heart Like a Sky*, which was not a good time for me.
I remember walking to Air Studios in Oxford Circus, where we were recording the new album. The sun was shining, it was a lovely day but, the closer I got to the studio, the more anxious and tense I felt. I told everyone I felt unwell and just walked straight back out again. I was stressed out; I'd had enough.

WORLD TOUR, 1989

Sadly, not one of the happiest periods of my career. Spandau were promoting our final album, *Heart Like a Sky*, with a world tour and the seams were starting to unravel.

Making this album took such a long time, cost a fortune and wasn't a pleasant experience. Hoping a residential trip would help, John suggested we go away together, where we could work all day then have dinner and a few beers, have a laugh and get the old vibe back. It didn't happen, though. Martin and Gary were working on the film *The Krays*, Steve had some personal issues and everything felt disjointed. Unfortunately we faffed about and went from one studio to another. We spent hours and hours deliberating over every note. It took almost a year to nail it.

By the time we went on tour the atmosphere wasn't great. We'd had some amazing times together, but this tour wasn't a happy one. There was a slow realisation that this could be the last hurrah for us as a band, and it was. We had run our course, at least until 2009.

MALIBU, 1992

After Spandau Ballet stopped working together, I recorded my first solo album, *The State of Play*, in Los Angeles. To promote the album we did a photoshoot in Malibu, which was a beautiful location. The sunsets there are stunning.

I had always liked American rock music and I had this vision of creating something similar. I went to the States and had a brilliant time, but I very quickly realised that it wasn't the album that I should be making. I'm not from LA, I'm from London!

I had fun hanging out in the bars, being with my band, meeting the bands Toto and Kiss and working with the superb producer Ron Nevison. However, I was worried about whether the album would connect; sadly, it didn't. The album was good, but the music didn't translate back in the UK. I found myself going back to basics, playing live and doing the clubs, as the singles we released weren't hits.

DUBAI, 1996

We did an amazing photoshoot in Dubai for my
second solo album, *Tony Hadley,* with Brian Aris. It
was primarily a covers album of classic hits, many
with quite quirky arrangements, produced by Gary
Stephenson. I particularly liked the Duran Duran song
'Save a Prayer', especially as my good friend Simon
Le Bon did backing vocals for me.

   We didn't have a massive budget for this job, and
we had to shoot three videos in a fairly short space
of time. I wanted somewhere hot, so we chose
Dubai, but no one (including me) had the good sense
to check the weather for July. Temperatures were
sizzling in the forties! Walking out of your hotel was
like walking into a furnace. After three days of filming,
members of the team were dropping like flies with
dehydration and tiredness. Fortunately we managed
to get hold of some rehydration sachets, and we all
perked up.

   We filmed in some gorgeous places: the desert,
in the markets and on boats. The colours and the
backdrops there are beautiful. A headshot of me
became the album cover, but I love these images,
especially the one of me falling back into the water.

KOSOVO, BOSNIA, THE FALKLAND ISLANDS, 1998–2000

(THIS PAGE AND OVERLEAF)

I am very proud to have been involved in the CSE (Combined Services Entertainment) shows. I have so much respect for the military; it was a real honour to perform for our troops.

On these tours there's normally a dancing troupe, a comedian and a magician or contortionist. Some of the off-stage events and experiences are mind-blowing. These pictures sum up amazing times for me. The Fabulous TH Band have been asked to entertain troops all around the world. We've been to places that most people would probably never get to visit such as Kosovo, the Falklands, Ascension Island, Kuwait and Bosnia. I would have loved to have gone to Afghanistan, but it was considered too perilous.

We were always given great hospitality after the shows. In Banja Luka, the officers, sergeants and regular soldiers really looked after us. We ended up in the SAS section. At the end of the night I had to be carried back to my accommodation by two SAS guys; I think I may have been a little bit worse for wear! With 3 ft of snow on the ground it was quite hard going for them.

We've been to Bosnia, armed with teddy bears to give out to the children in the street, but we needed to be accompanied by armed guards, front and back, which was quite scary.

One of the most dangerous places we visited was Northern Ireland, even after the Troubles. When we arrived at the base on the border there was a helicopter gun ship just above the base flying out with a 50-calibre machine gun. Half the barracks were fully loaded up with arms and weapons ready to go on patrol. The week before we arrived a mortar was thrown into the base, landing just above where we were playing that night! Luckily they managed to diffuse it.

When we went to the Falklands there was only one runway. If the wind was too strong you couldn't land. When our flight came in we had to be diverted to Ascension Island. Finally we got to the Falklands and the troops there were amazing; it was like being in Manchester or Liverpool on a Friday or Saturday night. It was a great atmosphere, one big party, and we went down a storm.

We got to do incredible things like visit Sea Lion Island. I'd never seen elephant seals before, let alone been so near one. It was so big and still I thought it was a rock. They are massive, about 12–15 ft long and 4 ft wide. The band couldn't believe how brave I was standing so close, but when it moved, no one had ever seen me run so fast in my life!

Playing football against the Gurkha regiment in the Falklands was very special, but a match in Kosovo against the military was just as memorable. The path we walked up had been de-mined and cleared of IEDs (Improvised Explosive Devices) so we thought we were fine. However, when the ball got kicked into the next field, which was fenced off, our bass player, Phil Williams, jumped over the fence to retrieve it. The military guys screamed at him not to move. That area hadn't been checked so they didn't know if it had mines in it. Phil had the ball and they told him to stay calm and retrace his steps. Luckily it had been snowing and he could see his footprints; that was a lifesaver.

During a trip to Kosovo we played to the NATO troops in an old cinema with barbed wire around it. The next day the show was cancelled because someone had been shot outside the cinema. Sometimes we were in places that were quite frightening.

**KOSOVO, BOSNIA, THE FALKLAND ISLANDS,
1998–2000**

Flying in military helicopters was one of my
favourite experiences. We first flew in one in
Kosovo and got to ramp ride in a Chinook which
was thrilling. The loading ramp is put down and
you attach yourself to a thin piece of wire and sit
there with your feet dangling in mid-air. All that's
between you and the ground is a tiny piece of cord.

In the Falklands I got to do a 'negative G'; you
drop an aircraft really quickly from the sky to
create a negative gravity, and you float in the air.

LONDON, 1999

This was a very difficult period for me, John and Steve. We'd tried to resolve the dispute over royalty payments amicably for years with our manager Steve Dagger, but we ended up suing Gary. The intricacies of the case have been well documented but going to court is not something you do lightly or on a whim. It was a horrible situation and a very messy feud.

What is so sad is how the relationship between five lads who started out in a school band, became good mates and went on to become one of the biggest and most successful pop bands of the 80s could become so broken. Our families were friends, our parents and children all knew each other well, we had travelled around the world and had fantastic times together. We were a very successful team.

It was a terribly stressful and expensive loss; twenty-three days in the High Court in London is not for the faint-hearted. We had good representatives who believed in our cause, but sadly the judge found in favour of Gary. When I heard we lost the case, it felt like a kick in the stomach.

That loss put a huge financial strain on the three of us. It was a hammer blow, but ultimately I have survived and evolved. Knock me down and I'll always get up again.

MACHU PICCHU TREK, 2003

My involvement in Action Medical Research came about through my manager, John Glover. Here I am with my great friend Brian Hornsby, who used to play for Arsenal. We're both in our football shirts! It's a brilliant charity that gives money to scientists to develop new technologies and vaccines. The Machu Picchu trek was with Brian, John and Matt Glover, and some of our friends. A lot of our fellow trekkers had been through life-changing experiences. They wanted to set themselves a challenge to help their recovery and raise money.

When you get off the plane at Cusco, the altitude hits you like a brick. It's so high and you are totally spaced out. You can't prepare for it; you can be as fit as anything but still succumb to altitude sickness. When we got to our hotel, our medics advised us to get an early night as we were starting very early in the morning. A quick breakfast was planned, then a long day trekking uphill at altitude. I didn't fancy that, I wanted to go out for a drink, so we hit the town. We went to a lively wine bar with music – and found the medics who had told us to get an early night! We were having a few drinks when a guy came up to me to say hello. I couldn't believe it: I was in the middle of Peru and a guy I used to play football with yonks ago was there too! We partied quite heavily that night but still got up for the trek.

The Peruvians who accompanied us were brilliant. They were very fit whereas we struggled a bit. On our way to the first site, I thought, wouldn't it be amazing if there was a bar up there? When we came to the open area where they were putting up the tents, lo and behold there was an old Peruvian woman with about thirty beers, keeping them cold in the river. I offered to buy them all!

You can do it the easy way and get the train up, but doing the trek is so rewarding. It takes three or four days, so it's quite strenuous. You can have someone carry your kit, which is about 75–80 lbs, but I wanted to carry it myself. It was tiring, but I like to be self-sufficient and do things properly. It was quite emotional getting to the top of Machu Picchu, and the whole trip was really inspiring. I've also trekked in Venezuela and the Costa Rican jungle. It's a great way to raise money for charity and have an incredible experience at the same time.

HYDE PARK, 2004

What an honour to be photographed by Lord Lichfield. He was so lovely and charming. We were doing a photoshoot for a magazine at the Serpentine in London's Hyde Park. It's a classic *Singin' in the Rain* image.

I'm totally at home on stage, I'm happy being interviewed and I enjoy making music videos, but I'm not that comfortable doing shoots, especially on my own. I'm very self-conscious. It's a bit easier being photographed when you're in a band. We had a saying in Spandau, 'Assume positions', and we all knew how we had to stand and who to lean on. As a solo artist I never know what to do with myself and so a prop is always a big help!

Lord Lichfield's enthusiasm and encouragement made it a fun shoot, and he got the shot he wanted very quickly.

SWING TOUR, 2006

I did a nationwide tour to promote the swing album *Passing Strangers*. Singing swing is a completely different style to conventional pop and rock; it takes a different vocal discipline. I love Frank Sinatra but tend to opt for a more Tony Bennett and Jack Jones style as some of Sinatra's keys are very low.

This is a special album for my mum as she and my late dad played so much of this music when I was a child. Growing up listening to that style of singing enabled me to pick it up quite naturally.

We covered songs on the album but not the obvious ones. However, on the live shows, it was nice to throw in a few Sinatra classics!

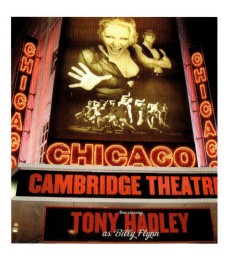

CHICAGO, 2007

I loved playing Billy Flynn in *Chicago* at London's Cambridge Theatre. Having my name up in lights on a West End stage was quite special.

I had been working on a swing album, *Passing Strangers*, for some time and when I was approached to play Billy I was thrilled. I'd never acted before or sung in a West End production, but I liked that it had a live band, and it was also perfect timing for promoting my album.

I went to see the show with my mum and Ali, and I loved it. I thought it would be easy as I had a small amount of dialogue and only three songs. It was not until I got the script that I realised how much there was to do. This was completely out of my comfort zone and I wondered what on earth I had let myself in for. I had no problems with the songs or learning the lyrics, but there was more acting than I thought there would be, and I also had to speak in an American accent. I used to wake up in the early hours to look at the script; I was so stressed about it. However, baby Zara was just two months' old, so it was a perfect time to be at home during the day.

On the first night I had never been more scared in my entire life. But I did it. I didn't fluff my lines and managed to pull off the American accent. The reviewers gave me four out of five stars, which was great.

Of course, I made a few mistakes, but it was a good laugh overall, and I made some wonderful friends. After checking in to the theatre I would pop into the pub opposite for a couple of drinks, and would go back again post-show. It was very jolly.

There were moments of sheer terror, though. One night I couldn't remember my next line, so I made it up. Someone in the wings was shouting the words at me but I was in a state of panic. It was a horrible feeling. Finally the line came to me and I don't think anyone in the audience noticed the fluff.

My two-and-a-half-month run was extended by a month. I felt a big sense of achievement. Doing a theatre production was a great experience and I'm so pleased I took the plunge.

WALES, 2008

Phil Taylor, our old keyboard player and still one of my great mates, suggested The Fabulous TH Band spend a week away to thrash out some songs. We had never done it before, and it was a great bonding experience. We stayed at a house in Wales owned by Phil's mate, and we all contributed to the music and writing. Spending uninterrupted time as a band adds to the camaraderie, as you get down time together too. We would either go out for dinner or cook in the big kitchen and have a few drinks. It's a great way to work on new material. Phil and I are pictured with Richie Barrett, our guitarist; Phil Williams on bass; and John Keeble on drums.

LONDON, 2009

We held a press conference on the *HMS Belfast* to announce we were getting back together and would be embarking on a world tour. We chose that location because we had played a gig there way back in 1979. We liked unusual venues when we started out, and playing on the ship had been hot, sweaty and exciting. We had felt we were on the verge of something really special and that great things were about to happen. After grafting from being a school band, we had finally felt that we were making some headway.

This is an historic picture because, as a fractured band, we had buried our demons. It was a great day, and we were in good spirits. The world's media were there. They didn't think we would ever get back together and I honestly didn't think we would either. Getting to that point was monumental.

Some time beforehand, I had made a flippant remark on my great friend Shane Richie's radio show when he asked if Spandau would ever get back together. I said that one day we might. The comment went viral and suddenly there was global interest in us reforming. John Keeble had a serious talk with me about how much the fans would love it; he thought we should give it another shot. I was reluctant at first, but after six months I felt ready to try. I had met up with all the other band members, but I still hadn't seen Gary. We met at The Flask, a pub in Highgate, and John sat between us in case we had a fight! It was quite a frosty meeting. Gary and I got a lot off our chests then agreed that if this was going to work we would have to put the past behind us. We shook hands, had a couple of pints and that was the new beginning.

DUBLIN, 2009 (PREVIOUS PAGE)

Twenty years after the band broke up, we were back
on stage together for the first time. This Dublin show
kicked off The Reformation Tour in Ireland and the UK.
Getting ready to go on stage was incredible; as we
stood behind the screen that showed our silhouettes,
the roar from the audience was thunderous. When the
curtains dropped the crowd erupted and we were into
the first song. It felt amazing to be back.

THE REFORMATION TOUR, 2009

Although it was a bit difficult at first, overall it felt great
to be reunited and back on stage together. We knew it
would never be exactly the same, but we were friends
again and we had some really good times on that tour.

WEDDING, 2009

Ali and I were married on 24 July 2009 at beautiful Cliveden House in Buckinghamshire. We'd fallen in love with Cliveden after I'd performed a couple of private shows there; its wood-panelled library was the perfect venue for exchanging our vows. Obviously it was my second marriage and, whilst it was a special day for us, we were aware of the sensitive nature of these events. So we decided to have a quiet ceremony with just our dear friends Ali and Nick Barber as our witnesses.

This was during the Spandau reunion, when we were working on an album – acoustic versions of the hits with a couple of new songs thrown in. The studio was just half an hour up the road from Cliveden. I had a window of two or three free days, so we planned to enjoy a relaxing lunch and spa day on the Friday and get married on the Saturday.

After the studio session on Thursday the lads suggested a few drinks to celebrate – a quiet stag do! The studio was residential, so we had a lovely meal with wine and a few beers. Later someone brought out the tequila and champagne and we started mixing it. Not a great idea. I called it a night at 2 am. When I arrived at Cliveden on Friday, Ali could definitely tell I'd had a few drinks the night before!

The ceremony was so beautiful and very emotional. I had a big speech ready, but I only managed to get halfway through before I was overwhelmed! A week later Ali and I threw a summer party at our favourite pub in Highgate for all our family and friends. It was a lovely sunny day and really relaxed, as most people didn't actually know the reason for the party until my father-in-law, Peter, delivered the perfect father-of-the-bride speech.

I love these pictures that remind us of a very special day. There's also this lovely photo of me and Ali with my mum, Jo, and Ali's parents, Margot and Peter. And then there's the brilliant photo of me and so many of my best friends.

We didn't have a honeymoon because the band was straight back in the studio, and then we went on tour for a year. We've had lots of lovely family holidays with our beautiful daughters, Zara and Genevieve, but the honeymoon is still pending!

US TOUR, 2011

There's a club in New York that hosts regular 80s nights, with stars from that era performing with the house band; they're hugely popular events and attract a really young audience. When I did a show there, I originally thought the 21-year-olds in the crowd wouldn't have a clue who I was, but I was so wrong: they knew the words to every hit. It was like I had gone back in time; it was great.

The band hired two SUVs and toured the south of America, including Las Vegas and Texas. Seven of us were drivers on that tour but as soon as I'm a passenger I nod off straight away. We split the band in two and drove through the desert for around seven hours a day. Touring sounds glamorous but it's hard work, back-to-back gigging and driving.

There's John Keeble, Phil Williams, Richie Barrett and Phil Taylor. We played in the main street opposite The Golden Nugget in Vegas and the audiences were amazing. All the band have children so we try not to be away from home for too long. Back in the Spandau days I would be away for three or four months, which was difficult; when travelling the States now, we do about four or five weeks.

GUINNESS WORLD RECORD, 2013

As part of Comic Relief, British Airways asked me, singer Kim Wilde, her brother Ricky Wilde and my guitarist Richie Barrett if we would come on board a Boeing-767 in an attempt to break the record for the highest electric performance in the sky. I believe the singer James Blunt had the record before us. The Guinness World Records adjudicator was on board and in charge of proceedings, and was told by the captain when we reached the height to break the record. We went up to 43,000 ft.

The flight was packed with 80s enthusiasts who were dressed up as stars like Cyndi Lauper and Freddie Mercury. We had to make sure that all the instruments were plugged into an amp but the problem was powering them. We needed so many batteries to give us enough power to perform for just a few minutes, but it worked – and we still hold the record!

ROYAL ALBERT HALL, LONDON, 2013
(THIS PAGE, PREVIOUS SPREAD AND NEXT TWO SPREADS)

This venue means so much to me. As well as our 1983 show, Spandau also played the Royal Albert Hall in 2014 for the premier of our film, *Soul Boys of the Western World*. I also sang there with Cliff Richard and Dionne Warwick for a World Hunger Day concert – and of course it's where I saw one of my all-time favourite singers, Frank Sinatra.

It's always a thrill to sing in that beautiful arena. Performing with my band, known as The Fabulous TH Band, is great. We've had a few changes in the line-up over the years, but the band is now Phil Williams on bass guitar and vocals, Richie Barrett on guitar and vocals, Lily Gonzalez on percussion and vocals, Tim Bye on drums, Adam Wakeman on keyboards and vocals, and when Adam's not available we have Tim Oliver and Sean Barry as perfect stand-ins. We have a fabulous brass section in Simon Willescroft on sax, and Dan Carpenter and Chris Storr on trumpets. The standard of musicianship is amazing. We have a lot of respect for each other and always enjoy performing together.

LONDON, 2014

Spandau Ballet were synonymous with London's Blitz club, a wine bar by day and flamboyant, avant garde club by night. The late Steve Strange used to run the door and decide whether people looked cool enough to be let in. The more he turned people away, the more outrageous the glitterati of London would look to try to get in. He even turned away Mick Jagger once, which we thought was madness.

The original days of the Blitz was a great era for new fashion and new music; the New Romantic look was huge. We became the musical focus for the club. When you thought of Blitz, you thought of Spandau Ballet in a similar way that when you thought of the Rum Runner in Birmingham you thought of Duran Duran. It was a wonderful trip down memory to lane to unveil the plaque for the location of our first gig.

FILM PREMIERE, 2014

To promote *Soul Boys of the Western World*, a documentary about our journey as a band, we played the Royal Albert Hall, which was as special as ever. We also travelled to Rome and Barcelona, doing interview after interview. It felt good; as a group we were in a happy place.

It's hard to remember a time when social media wasn't at our fingertips, but we didn't have personal video equipment or mobile phones back in the 80s. So to make the film, producer Scott Millaney and director George Hencken had to delve deep into the archives. We managed to get so much footage, which was fantastic.

George was very direct. She said it had to be down to her to best represent Spandau Ballet, and insisted that no one in the band or management manipulate the film. We all accepted that she was in charge, and I think she did a sterling job. It's a brutally honest film that I found quite difficult to watch. On one hand it captures the euphoric early days and on the other you can see the slow deterioration within the group. There are moments where you can feel the tension.

It's quite intense revisiting your younger, glory days. My dad and grandad were in it too, and it's sad seeing people on film who are no longer with you. I've watched it three times, and it may be a while before I watch it again!

TEXAS, 2014

We went to the States to promote *Soul Boys of the Western World* at South by Southwest in Austin, Texas, which is a big film, media and music festival.

We were all in good spirits; we were in a country we loved and it was the early stages of promoting the film. Everything felt fresh and exciting. It was great performing at SXSW and also hanging out with other bands and musicians.

I was also happy because I got to eat amazing brisket – and you can't beat American brisket!

LONDON, 2015

Meeting Her Majesty The Queen was an absolute highlight for me.

I was at Buckingham Palace attending a champagne reception held for people who fundraise for charity. I have been involved with many charities over the years, but I'm very close to Shooting Star Children's Hospices, who I was representing at this event. They support families with children whose health conditions mean they are not expected to reach the age of 19. I've worked with their Executive Vice President and my dear friend, Karen Sugarman MBE, for many years to raise money and awareness for this exceptional cause, along with our Royal Patron, Sophie, Countess of Wessex, and my fellow Vice Presidents Dame Joan Collins and Simon Cowell.

It's really lovely to see these pictures again as the whole event was a blur. I was so nervous – I still can't remember what we spoke about! I wanted to pinch myself. I couldn't believe I was meeting the Queen; I was so proud.

I could only stay for about half an hour after speaking with her as I had a car outside waiting to take me to Germany to join the Spandau boys for a breakfast TV interview. My driver Chris sped through the night to the ferry, then drove for hours across Europe, looking after me and keeping me entertained. It was one of those memorable journeys. I turned up at the studio having had no sleep, but after a load of make-up was slapped on me, I got through the interview and a vocal performance. I was exhausted!

I have had some ups and downs in life but on the whole I'm very lucky and happy. Not everyone is as fortunate, so I do whatever I can to help others. If I can sing a few songs to raise much-needed funds, I will.

A further proud moment for me was being awarded an MBE in the 2020 New Year Honours List for my charitable work. I have been unable to receive the actual honour yet, due to the pandemic, but hope to be able to do so this summer. When I opened the letter I was stunned but delighted. My whole family were so thrilled for me. I'm very grateful and extremely honoured.

VERONA, 2015

This is a beautiful venue, the Verona
Arena. It was an incredible honour to sing
in a space where greats such as Pavarotti
and Plácido Domingo have performed
and where operas have been staged. The
structure of the amphitheatre means you
can't play ridiculously loud, but the sound
quality was excellent – the Romans got it
right! It's a great place to play, and I love
the colours in this picture.

WORLD TOUR, 2015

The *Soul Boys of the Western World* film was the peg for the World Tour which took in much of Europe, America and South East Asia. Touring is always hard work, with lots of travelling, but it's an amazing experience and one that I love.

I'm enjoying one of my favourite meals, a giant seafood platter, in Gladstones, Santa Monica. I love Los Angeles and always try to go to this restaurant when I'm in town. It's a bit rough and ready but the food is fab.

My other favourite restaurants include Marix, a great Tex-Mex joint, and Barney's Beanery is always on the list too, a chilled restaurant and bar where you can shoot some pool and drink fine craft beers. I always have a great time in the States. Everything is larger than life. The larger the better.

WORLD TOUR, 2015

John wasn't in this picture of us enjoying a fantastic Chinese meal in Hong Kong; sadly he was taken ill. The restaurant was down by the docks where they brought in the fish fresh off the boats. This one was recommended to us as one of the best. You didn't get to choose from a menu, the chef and his team just kept bringing out dish after dish. It was incredible food.

This could be called our 'last supper' as it was towards the end of the tour, and I told the guys that I wouldn't be carrying on with them. They wanted to extend the tour but I had my own commitments. I had done a year and a half with the band doing performances, promotional work and appearances, but I had a solo album to finish and the TH Band had been waiting for months to start working again. The conversation didn't go down too well; there was a bit of an atmosphere afterwards.

ITALY, 2015 (THIS SPREAD AND OVERLEAF)

I love this quirky image, which was for the front cover of *The Christmas Album*. I was on tour in Europe with Spandau and we were playing lots of dates in Italy. We all did what we wanted on our days off, and I would get a train or plane to Milan to work on the album.

I wore a bespoke red suit for the cover shoot, which made for a lovely Christmassy feel against the white backdrop. The model, who was very attractive, had her face covered with a bauble, which was quite bizarre, and nobody got to see her in the album photos. So I wanted to include the photo of us in reverse in this book as she's a hell of a lot better looking than me! It was a fun photoshoot, and the images are very stylish, with an Italian magazine feel to them.

I'M A CELEBRITY… GET ME OUT OF HERE!, 2015

I'm a massive fan of *I'm A Celeb…* and watch it every year; the celebrities eating disgusting things always make me laugh. ITV had asked me to do the show several times, but it never felt like the right moment. But after a year and a half with Spandau Ballet I knew I would go off and finish my album *Talking to the Moon*, so I agreed to do it; it was a great way to tell people that I was back as a solo performer.

I wasn't particularly fazed about entering the Australian jungle as I had already done many treks for Action Medical Research, where I would carry 70 lbs of kit for hours, so I thought a few trials and laying around in a hammock would be a walk in the park.

I had such a fun time, despite the well-documented arguments with Lady Colin Campbell! It all started off OK and I was very respectful to her. I even gave her my bed and slept on the floor. But she wasn't the easiest to get on with. Everyone else was great company, though, and I especially hit it off with Duncan Bannatyne; we became good mates.

What you see on TV is real, especially the hunger. The rice and beans are so bland and any portions of protein like crocodile or kangaroo are tiny. After a few days you're starving. I lost 20 lbs in three-and-a-half weeks! When you see campmates drooling over a piece of chocolate, it's because we were craving something sweet so much. When my team won a banquet in a task, we eagerly dug into the mountain of exquisite food and alcohol, but we felt sick pretty quickly. We lay around in a food coma and slept for hours. When you do fill your face after eating very little for weeks it's a real shock to the system.

You don't get any help with anything; you have to build your own cooking area and somewhere to dry your clothes. It's really hard to dry your socks in the jungle. I actually got trench foot, as well as an ear and throat infection, and was on antibiotics for two weeks when I got home.

Before you go in, a psychologist checks your mental health and assesses whether the experience could be too daunting. I told them I wasn't afraid of heights, snakes or rats, so doing the trials wouldn't bother me. A lot of the celebrities had phobias and got really het up about the trials. Missing home also affected some quite badly; the tears were real. I just reminded myself that Ali and my three girls who had travelled to Australia were at the Versace Hotel, sunbathing by the pool in December, so they were fine!

Celebrities voted out early stay at the hotel until the end. I lasted until the last five. I'm glad I stayed in so long, but I was very happy to get a couple of days at the Versace! A cameraman told me that when I slept on the floor, they needed a camera on me all night. I didn't close my sleeping bag so they had to check no snakes were slithering in!

The psychologist speaks to you after the show to assess how the experience has affected you and if you need any emotional support. They were reassured when I told them I'd had a great time, and I was off to get a very cold bottle of white wine and a massive burger with all the trimmings. In all, it was brilliant. I loved every minute of it and would do it again if I had the chance.

THE NETHERLANDS, 2016

I'm in my element here. We got to visit the European Space Research and Technology Centre (ESTEC), based just outside Amsterdam, which helps with the development of Europe's space capability. It's a remarkable project.

I have always been fascinated by science, and I especially love anything to do with UFOs and aliens. I enjoy reading about space. All very different to the musical side of my life. Though I did name one of my albums *Talking to the Moon* as I often stare up into the sky and wonder what is going on out there!

The band was touring Europe in a sleeper bus and were playing in Amsterdam for one night. We thought we might get tickets to ESTEC, but when my manager, Matt (third on the left), contacted the venue, it was closed for visitors that day. I was so chuffed when they said they would open for a private tour. I would have happily queued for hours, so this was a totally unexpected treat. We got to speak to a Dutch and a British scientist, who were absolutely fascinating.

Lily and I are mucking about, 'floating' in the space capsule. I just wish I could do that for real!

THE BAND, 2016

These guys deserve a special mention. They are fabulous – that's why I call them The Fabulous TH Band.

So many people associate me with Spandau Ballet, and that's fine. However, I've been a solo artist for the vast majority of my career. I'm lucky enough to work with amazing musicians who are also very happy and upbeat.

Not only are these guys fantastic musicians they are also very good friends. I ask their opinion and advice and we write together. It's a very inclusive set-up.

We are professional when it comes to performing but we like to have fun too. There's none of this 'no drinking before a gig' malarkey! Before we go on stage our ritual is to drink a '99', which is 99 per cent alcohol and 1 per cent mixer. Richie Barrett makes a funny quip related to the day, we knock the drinks back in one, put the glasses upside down on our heads and then we're on!

My management team, John Glover, Matt Glover and Heidi Herdman, and all the crew are brilliant. I'm surrounded by good people and that is so important in this business. It can be a nasty industry and you want people around you who you can trust.

Messing around here is Tim Bye, Phil Taylor (who isn't with us now as he's working on production and writing, but we're still great pals), me, Lily Gonzalez, Phil Williams and Richie.

GARDEN PARTY, 2017

Here's the Fabulous TH Band gang and their partners at a party in our garden a couple of years ago. We haven't been able to do this sort of gathering for a while, but I can't wait to have everyone over again as soon as possible. We fire up the barbeque, eat and drink as much as we want and let our hair down. Most of us have young children, so they all come too. We have a fun day hanging out together and having a bit of a party. It's just a way for me to thank them all.

LET'S ROCK, 2017 (THIS PAGE AND OVERLEAF)

Let's Rock is a fun, family friendly, retro festival that's been growing each year, with more and more venues across the country. The audience is always amazing; everyone is there for a really good time. The fans that came to gigs in the 80s now bring their children with them to these shows, so there are a lot of young people in the audience. They seem to know the words to every song. We'll always do a Queen track like 'We Are the Champions' because I'm a massive fan of the band and it's a real crowd-pleaser. The fans really do like to rock.

For me, one of the best things about doing these festivals is meeting up with other musicians. There's a lovely camaraderie backstage among the performers.

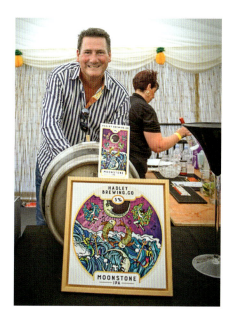

LET'S ROCK, 2017

I served some of my own beer at Let's Rock this year. A lovely company had suggested they make a beer for me, and we ended up with Hadley's Gold. I loved the concept and then got involved with The Great Yorkshire Brewery and designed Moonstone IPA. The beer was 5 per cent and went down very smoothly and easily. I enjoyed the whole process, going to the brewery, meeting the guys who made the beer – and I especially liked drinking it! It was an interesting venture and I'm glad I did it, but music takes up so much of my time that sadly I couldn't continue down the hops route!

BERLIN, 2019

I absolutely love Germany and we like to perform there as often as we can, sometimes twice a year. And our German fans have been spreading the word. We started off playing in small clubs and now we've made real headway there and are selling out larger venues.

Spandau were reasonably big in Germany but not as popular as in Italy or Spain. I love being in Berlin; it's such a cool city. I never get tired of playing there.

AUSTRALIA AND JAPAN, 2020

The vibe in Japan is so different to anywhere else. The audiences are super enthusiastic. They have every album, every single; they are real collectors. The crowd is very polite when you're playing then cheer like mad and wave their albums between songs. We've played over there a few times and we are trying to build on our fan base. I'm very excited to play there again, later in 2022.

Australia is such a great country. I always say that if it took four hours to get there from the UK instead of twenty-four, everyone would want to live there! The crowds are fun, the atmosphere is always happy and the sun shines nearly all the time. What's not to like?! It also holds special memories for me as my little boy, Tom, who's now 38, took his first steps there when he and Leonie came out on Spandau's 1985 tour.

We were leaving Australia for Miami to pick up a festival cruise ship and this was one of our last meals together for a long time. We found a lovely restaurant on the coast, which was glorious. Working with The Fabulous TH Band is a real pleasure as we all enjoy socialising and have a good laugh when we go out. We spent around nine days on the cruise ship, came home and that was it: the world went into lockdown. This was our last get together for many months.

We tried to remain optimistic throughout lockdown with our weekly Zoom get-togethers. Every Tuesday night the whole team, band, management and crew, got online with a beer or glass of wine. We stayed in touch throughout which was important for morale. But we couldn't have been happier when we finally got to meet up and start playing gigs again.

CREDITS

Page 5: Steve Rapport/Getty Images

Pages 14, 17, 20, 23, 24, 25, 29, 31, 32, 39, 40, 50: Graham Smith

Pages 18, 19, 57, 58, 59, 60, 61, 62, 63, 64, 66, 68, 70, 75, 82: Mirrorpix

Page 26: Virginia Turbett/Redferns

Pages 34, 35, 69: Brian Cooke/Redferns

Pages 36, 37, 41, 54, 55, 73, 90, 93: Neil Mackenzie Matthews

Pages 44, 45, 46, 49, 53: Martyn Goddard

Page 74: Ron Bell

Pages 76, 78, 98, 99: Brian Aris

Page 80: Steve Hurrell/Redferns

Page 83: Pete Still/Redferns

Pages 84, 89: Denis O'Regan

Pages 86, 87: Shelley Watson/Getty Images

Page 94: David Redfern/Redferns

Page 96: Paul Harris/Getty Images

Pages 101, 102, 103, 104, 105, 108, 109, 112, 113, 114, 116,
117, 122, 123, 126, 127, 128, 138, 139, 140, 142, 143, 147,
148, 149, 153, 156, 157, 158, 166, 172, 173: Matt Glover

Pages 106, 107: Shutterstock

Page 110: Lichfield Archive/Getty Images

Page 119: Samir Hussein/Getty Images

Page 121: Brian Rasic/Getty Images

Pages 124, 125: Jeff Krotz

Pages 130, 131, 132, 134, 137: Christie Goodwin

Page 141: Dave J Hogan/Getty Images

Pages 144, 145: Chris Radburn/WPA Pool/Getty Images

Page 148 (top right): Jeff Golden/WireImage

Pages 154, 155: Shutterstock

Pages 160, 161, 162: Martin Shaw

Page 165: Frank Hoensch/Redferns

Page 175 (top left): Dave Hogan/Getty Images

Co-author Linda Udall is a journalist who co-wrote the
bestselling *Saved* with Peter and Steph Shilton. She was
formerly Deputy Features Editor at *Sunday People* and *Yes!*
and a features writer at *Rosemary Conley Diet and Fitness*
magazine and Chelsea FC's official magazine.

ACKNOWLEDGMENTS

Thank you so much to everyone for making this wonderful picture book happen.

Firstly, I'd like to thank my friend Harry Harris for encouraging me to create this book.
Massive thanks to journalist Linda Udall, Harry's wife, who has been incredibly patient listening
to my stories and anecdotes, and transcribing them to make the photos come to life.

Big thanks to all at Omnibus Press, especially managing editor David Barraclough
and his indomitable fellow editor Imogen Gordon Clark! Thank you for your patience.
Thanks to Lora Findlay for the book design, and David Stock, Greg Morton
and Debra Geddes for their work on the marketing and publicity.

Thank you to all the brilliant photographers whose work over
the years has captured so many wonderful images that have taken me
and hopefully you to another dimension. Such great artists!

Thanks to my brilliant management team John Glover, Matt Glover,
Julie Glover and Heidi Herdman of Blueprint Management. We've been great pals
and work colleagues for many years and there's never a dull moment!
Matt, thanks for searching high and low for so many amazing pictures.

Thank you to the boys in Spandau Ballet, so many incredible images
and fantastic memories from the past!

To the Fabulous TH Band and all the crew who've been with me through thick and thin:
I can't thank you enough!

Last but not least thanks to my wonderful family and friends,
including my wife, Ali, daughters Toni, Zara and Genevieve and my sons Tom and Mack.
Anyone who thinks it's easy being with someone in the music industry is mistaken –
it's a tough and often selfish business and I thank you for your love and resilience!

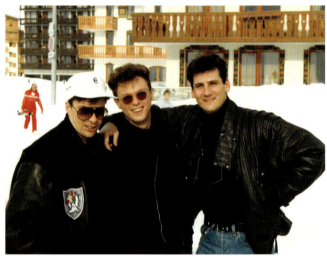

FUN

I hope you've enjoyed this glimpse into my world. There is so much amazing imagery in this book, but I couldn't resist sneaking in some of my own photo album favourites.

[Clockwise from left] In my 'budgie smugglers' in Jamaica having caught a barracuda. I was just 22 – you wouldn't catch me in a pair of trunks like that now!

With Gary and John on a TV shoot in France. As soon as I got the chance I grabbed a pair of skis and was off on the slopes.

Fishing with Ali in Mauritius. It's a beautiful island and where we first met. I loved being on that boat. I look very excited!

[Clockwise from right] At Arsenal's Emirates Stadium, with actor Ralf Little, former Arsenal players Danny O'Shea and Steve Williams, ex-Chairman the late Peter Hill-Wood, former Arsenal player Brian Hornsby and Arsenal's community programme director Alan Sefton MBE. I'm a big Gunners fan so it was great to be on the hallowed turf for an awards presentation.

Very pleased with my catch of the day!

On a skiing holiday with Ali, having a break and a nice glass of wine. Skiing is one of our favourite holidays with all the children, who are all very good skiers. We have a fantastic time together, and I can't wait to get back on the slopes with them again.

FUNNY WHO YOU BUMP INTO!

When you set off on your path to becoming a musician all you dream about is performing and getting a hit record. Music is your life. Once you're successful it opens so many doors. I've always said I'm incredibly lucky to get paid for doing something I love while also having so much fun. You get thrown into the crazy world of showbiz and meet some amazing people. This selection shows just a few of the great memories I have with some very special people…

[Above] Spandau with DJs Chris Evans and Ken Bruce and two of my idols, Iggy Pop and John Cleese.

[Right from top] The lovely Lorraine Kelly, who really is lovely.

My long-time, very good pal Shane Richie joined me on stage at the Royal Albert Hall. We sang 'Do It for Love' by Hall & Oates for Children in Need. He's a great guy.

Messing about with the famous Italian rapper Caparezza, who is an incredibly talented man. He's huge in Italy. I recorded the track 'Goodbye Malinconia' with him which went to number one in the iTunes chart over there.

My mum, Jo, and my manager Matt's mum, Sue, with the legendary Tony Bennett. Our mums were thrilled to meet their musical hero, and so was I.

With Rick Astley who I've known for years, great friend Gary Barlow and the hilarious 'Chatty Man' Alan Carr and lovely Melanie Sykes.

With singer Beverley Knight and Heaven 17 singer Billie Godfrey.

FAMILY

I'm incredibly lucky to be blessed with such a wonderful family, and so I'd like to dedicate these pictures to them for all their love and support.

[Above] What a beautiful picture this is, with all five of my children together: Zara, Mackenzie, Tom, Toni and Genevieve.

[Opposite, left column, top to bottom] Lifting little Tom up after a Spandau concert. I think he must have been terrified; Mack celebrating his fifth birthday with Tom, Toni and Leonie; me with Toni, Tom and Mack.

[Opposite, middle column, top to bottom] Me and Ali with Zara and Genevieve; helping baby Tom in the pool; with Ali, her sister Elaine, and the girls on holiday in Portugal.

[Opposite, right, top to bottom] My mum and Ali in Times Square – they look very happy, for some reason; me and Ali with baby Zara; doing a zip wire run in the Lake District with Zara and Genevieve.